T0159087

The
STRUGGLE
with
STRUGGLE

The STRUGGLE with STRUGGLE

PASTOR WILLIAM A. BENNETT

authorHOUSE®

AuthorHouse™
1663 Liberty Drive
Bloomington, IN 47403
www.authorhouse.com
Phone: 1-800-839-8640

Published by AuthorHouse   08/28/2012

ISBN: 978-1-4772-6541-3 (sc)
ISBN: 978-1-4772-6542-0 (e)

Library of Congress Control Number: 2012915980

INTRODUCTION

How in the world did I get here? How have I become consumed by storms that once had no power over me? How can I have faith after doubt has seemingly defeated my hope? My heart wants to trust in God, but my mind is flooded with so many concerns and worries that I can no longer distinguish between the voice of God and the voice of my enemy. The darkness surrounds me both day and night, sleep eludes my eyelids, and rest betrays me because of my anxiety. How did I become so weak and fragile when I once stood sure in strength and grace? My vision has become as a man stricken in age, my dreams have become constant nightmares, and my voice, once a boisterous roar, has become a whisper too silent to hear. I have ignored the encouragement of others while giving agreement to those who point out my faults. I have become my greatest condemner.

And yet, I daily arise from the ashes of guilt and shame; I rise from the report that says death; and I speak life. I kneel to a God I struggle to believe, and without wavering, pray his mercy and grace over my life. I place one foot in front of the other, and in weakness I press to the mark that has been laid before me. Through darkness I stir up the faith that causes optimism and hope that causes belief. Though a wounded soldier, I put on the whole armor of God, and I fight with whatever strength I have. I find myself clutching the edge of the cliff and refusing to let go, while announcing to those around me that God will make a way. I open the Word of God and connect with its power, then I proceed to deliver to others what I have received of myself: the recipe of defeating defeat.

THE STRUGGLE WITH STRUGGLE

What is struggle? I would say the short definition is that it's the tug-of-war between our desires and our challenges. The only reason we have struggles is because things challenge our desires, making it hard for them to be fulfilled. If a single woman desires a relationship but lacks one, at some point if that desire lingers she will struggle with loneliness. In contrast, a single woman who has no desire for a relationship will not struggle with loneliness due to a lack of companionship because she doesn't desire it. If a man is hungry and desires food but doesn't have the means to obtain it, his struggle will be with how to find fulfillment relative to his hunger. In contrast, if a man has an abundance of food, his struggle will not be how to obtain what he already has. Essentially we desire based on our struggles, and we struggle based on the unfulfillment of our desires. Wouldn't it be nice if we could fulfill our desires without struggle? Sadly, that is not the case. We must realize and accept that struggle is a part of life and the enemy of our desires; wherever you find desire, somewhere close you will find struggle. For example, we desired freedom because of the struggle of slavery.

We establish laws because of the struggle with crime. Our struggles bring out the best of our desires, and although we dislike struggle, it is necessary in a way to point out our greatest needs. Our struggle with sin points to our great need for God's mercy and forgiveness. Truthfully, we didn't need sin to know God loved us, for he showed his love in his willingness to create us and keep us from sin. Yet is it not also true that because of our struggle with sin we now know that God's love for us extends to measures beyond our understanding? Because of sin, we recognize that God loves us even when we are a hot mess; furthermore, God's desire to love and redeem us caused him to give his own life.

Essentially what I'm saying is that the struggle with struggle is that unfortunately it's a part of our desire, so if we embrace our desires we must learn to embrace our struggles. Now this may seem a little extreme to you, and you're not ready to get used to struggle. Well, let me first say I'm not telling you to get used to struggle; I'm saying to accept the fact that struggle is connected to desires. When you accept that, you can let go of the shock and awe factor and begin the process of coping and overcoming.

The Bible is full of stories in which there was a desire or destination. Before the destination is reached, struggle appears, seemingly to prevent the desire. For instance, the apostle Paul states that he must go back to Jerusalem and stand before Caesar, but at the same time he says that the Holy Ghost revealed to him that bonds and afflictions await him when he gets there. So while Paul has a destination, he also has a struggle applied to the destination, but his reply was that none of those factors moved him or caused him to turn back. Peter, wanting to be sure that it was Jesus walking on the water, requested that the Lord allow him to do the same. When Jesus said, "Come," amazingly, Peter began to walk on the same water. But although Peter had a desire to step out of the boat and walk on the water, attached to this desire was also a storm that caused Peter to sink. If you don't accept the struggle but instead bow to it, then ultimately you forsake the desires by letting the struggle have the victory.

Jesus had a desire to redeem man; therefore, he embraced the cross and death to give life to his passion. The embracing of our struggles is nothing more than a commitment to overcome them. How committed are you to overcoming your struggle? Does your commitment to overcoming have a timetable attached to it? If the struggle isn't over by the time you set, will you then fold and allow struggle to kill your desire? I am a firm believer that desires can live through any struggle if the individual is willing to never fold while in the struggle. The commitment to overcoming your struggle must be unwavering, because the fact is that most struggles don't end overnight. Please don't allow the fear of your struggle to freeze your faith and the active commitment you have toward defeating your struggle.

Consider for a moment the Word of God and the great cloud of witnesses who endured struggles that seemed to have no end. And yet, they overcame. Perhaps the best example was Abraham, the father of Israel, who was seventy-five years old with no seed when God made him and his wife a promise. Abraham's desire of a seed was met with the struggle of his wife's womb being barren. The struggle was so bad that Abraham's wife laughed when she heard the promise of a seed; further, she encouraged Abraham to have a child with her maid because her own womb was dead. Struggle almost defeated the blessing and desire of a child, but God continued to encourage Abraham and assure him that his wife would bear seed as long as they committed to seeing it come to pass. Twenty-five years later, the seed that was trapped in struggle was birthed in victory. Similarly, the biblical woman with the issue of blood was sick for twelve long years; nothing was working, and everything was getting worse. Yet she determined that she was not going to allow the length of her struggle or pessimism to destroy her desire to be healed. This woman made up in her mind she would fight the struggle with faith and pressed through the crowd to get to Jesus. Many lessons are to be learned from her story, but perhaps the greatest is to not allow the struggle's duration to defeat your desire. I suggest that if we learn to embrace the struggle, at its end the desire will be worth more. Anything that costs more is worth more, and the more you have to struggle to get something, the greater it's worth after the struggle. If we would stop getting so caught up in the fact that we're in a struggle and focus on the fight to defeat the struggle, we would reach the desire much sooner. Here is something you must know: the struggle isn't trying to be homeless. It wants to live with you as long as you will allow it. If I were you I would totally commit to defeating what has being withholding your desires from coming to pass and serve your struggles with an eviction notice.

You don't have to get rid of the desire; you have to get rid of the struggle. Don't waste your time struggling with the fact that you have a struggle—spend your time defeating the struggle you have. Don't allow your desire to die while you fight for it to live; you must keep it alive until it can breathe on its own. Don't make it so easy for something you want to escape the grip of your reality. Just know that getting your desire in a later season is better than never getting it at all.

BAD, BETTER, GREATER

A gardener plants a small seed into the ground and then walks away from where he laid the seed. Why doesn't he stay at the place of that seed and wait a few hours for it to produce? The gardener understands that nothing begins in its full potential and that in order for the seed to grow into its purpose, it must first go through a process, and other elements such as sun and water must be applied. There is no need for him to watch the seed hours after it's been planted, for he understands you don't go from a small seed to a great harvest in hours.

A couple has been trying for a while to have a child. They are feeling optimistic this time as the wife goes to the doctor. The doctor administers the pregnancy test, and after about ten minutes lets the wife know the magic words: "You're pregnant." Why doesn't the doctor tell the woman at that point to lie back and prepare to deliver the baby? Obviously, the doctor understands that the point of conception is not the time for birthing, so he sends the woman home with instructions on how to take care of her body for several more months. The birthing of a child is a process: if you birth before it is time, you stand to risk the baby's good health and even life.

Likewise, how is it that we derive great expectations from bad positions? How is it that we desire no process to get from bad to great, from hurt to joy, from broke to rich? Why is it that we want the microwave as opposed to the stove when it comes to our pursuit of happiness and success? David said, before I got to the prepared table, before my cup started running over, I was in the valley of the shadow of death (Psalms 23). You don't go from death to overflow without a process. I believe that we hinder our greatness by rushing the process. We skip steps and end up slipping when trying to go too fast. We have to get to a point of understanding that if we're in a bad place, "better" comes before "greater." Even though greater is the ultimate desire, better is not to be ignored, for better is greater than bad.

A man just had surgery. The doctor says, "Take these pain pills because you are going to be in a lot of pain." He checks on his patient daily, re-wraps his bandage, and manages his pain with meds. Every day that the doctor sees his patient, he says, "I know you're in a lot of pain now, but it will get better with time." A week or so later he enters the man's hospital room, and his patient greets him by saying, "Doctor, I feel a whole lot better." No, the patient doesn't feel great yet or totally healed, but he recognizes that from the time of his surgery until now, the level of pain has improved. Whatever situation you're in, get better before you get greater. People lacking financially are generally in a rush to get rich, and when riches do not come quickly enough, the wait penetrates and causes an even deeper hole of disappointment and realization of how broke they are. If those same people focused on getting better before getting richer, they would at least get out of being broke even if they have not yet gotten rich. If you can say it's getting better, then you are doing something right. If it's staying the same while you're waiting on it to get greater, you're definitely doing it wrong.

Don't get me wrong: I'm not suggesting by any stretch of the imagination that God can't take you from one extreme to the next without going step-by-step. I believe that circumstances can actually change overnight, but the truth is those situations are few and far between. Every extreme makeover has to go through a process before the makeover is complete. In fact, when we wait on God to take us from bad to great, we waste so much time because God is actually waiting on us to go step-by-step. The Word of God encourages us to not despise the day of small things, because small things amount to great things. We must also understand that God is a process God: he took six days to create the world; he told Naaman, a leper, to dip himself in the Jordan seven times before he was healed; and he told Israel to encompass Jericho seven days before the walls came down. If we don't come to terms with the process of growth then we will stay in the same condition far longer than we want to.

We do ourselves a great disservice when we don't have a reasonable expectation of how long the process should take before it comes to an end. We have mastered the prolonging of pain by not properly tending to wounds because we simply desire that there be no pain. If someone is wounded, the wound must heal before there can be any real expectation of no pain as a result of the wound. Thus, how can a wound heal if the wounded refuses to go through a process of healing, but instead opts to escape the pain any way they can? As a pastor I have counseled many hurting people with deep wounds. The trend I've discovered is that most want answers on how to *not* feel the pain rather than answers about how to heal. Consequently we seek temporary fixes to not feel the pain and give little, if any, attention to healing the wound that's causing the pain. A temporary fix doesn't eliminate pain but causes you to forget it's there—at least until that fix is over, and the pain is back.

Many of us have become addicted to the fix and thus have lived year after year with wounds that have never healed.

A tornado sweeps through your city and destroys the great house that took you years to build. No matter the pain of the loss or the desire to have a great house again, the house can't be rebuilt the day that it was destroyed; you now must go through a process of rebuilding. The process of rebuilding doesn't make the value of the house any less once it's rebuilt. In fact, the way you must look at it is there is no value is a house destroyed. So why not go through a process that will eventually give the house its great value once again? Yes, it will be great when that house is rebuilt, but we can't ignore that the finished product is not the only beauty in the process. The simple cleaning and removal of the destroyed house from the land is better than the sight of the catastrophe. Plus, how can you rebuild if the destruction is still present? Even before a foundation is laid or one nail applied, there must be a blueprint. But a blueprint view is better than no view at all. When the builders begin to build the house there will first be a shell without walls, but there is beauty in the shell because you can see where the walls will go and the progress that is being made. Essentially what I'm saying is that you don't have to wait to get the great house to feel better about the destroyed house; as you go through the process you must celebrate the progress.

The better in your life doesn't have to take a backseat to the great; however, the better should precede the great. Pain is more tolerable when I'm fine with getting better, and while I'm waiting on becoming totally healed. I'm not going to try to get over a broken heart a day after the break, but daily I'll try to get better until I get to a place of total healing. Again, it has to be more than words: you have to be committed to the process of going from bad to better. Your family situation or relationship may be in bad shape, but don't let your expectation of total restoration cause you to neglect your commitment to getting better daily. Whatever the situation may be, work to make it better, believe in the process, and watch the end result be greater.

LET'S GET REAL

Struggle's greatest friend and companion is called "denial." Denial is the fuel that drives your struggle: the more you deny, the greater the struggle becomes. If you are in denial you empower your struggle, for you can never conquer what you won't admit.

There may be nothing worse than a parent watching their child struggle with an addiction to drugs. The addiction to drugs alone is itself a giant obstacle to overcome, but add denial and it becomes an impossible fight. The first thing that parents must do if they want to help their child is to get the child to admit that he has a problem and needs help. With that said, let's get real.

There seems to be some kind of hidden doctrine of the church that says "expose the beautiful parts of you and hide the messy." This doctrine says that you are acceptable as long as you don't have any faults, and you are an outcast if you do have faults. This doctrine has caused many to lose faith in the church as well as feel that they have to deny their struggle for fear that they will be judged as opposed to helped. Fortunately, this is not the doctrine of Christ. He reaches his hand out to those trapped in darkness and says, "Come with me, and you no longer have to hide." The Word of God says that Christ loved us while we were yet a sinner, which means he didn't wait for us to say "sorry" before he died. Christ didn't wait for us to put all of our childish ways aside before he called us. Instead he destined us, knowing at times we would fail. He reminds us in his Word that all have sinned and come short of the glory of God; he confronts us while making forgiveness available to us all. God says, "Come unto me all ye that labor and are heavy laden and I will give you rest," so let there be no doubt that God is not afraid of your struggle, nor is he asking you to hide. Anyone who makes you afraid to expose your weakness is your enemy, because that fear could be the very thing stopping you from getting free.

I'm amazed by and thankful for Paul, one of the greatest apostles who ever lived, because he risked his popularity when he exposed his issues. Throughout the Bible, Paul mentions the struggles he had and things that he had to learn, but this is what makes him great. He reminds us that he is human while anointed. Personally I can't stand those who portray anointing at the expense of denying their humanity. Paul lets us know that if you work at your humanity it doesn't have to get in the way of your anointing.

Before I can ask you to swim in realness I guess I have to dive in that pool myself. I can assure you of this one very thing: like Paul I have many faults, struggles, and insecurities, and if it hadn't been for God loving me through it all I would have been consumed by them. I found out quickly that hiding and denying doesn't serve to help the situation; it just prolongs the suffering that will come at some point. As a pastor I've learned that no matter how anointed I think I am, I still have weaknesses, ways, and thoughts that are not godly. Yes, I have tried to deny them, but as I found out quickly, that only makes things worse. So what am I to do? I'm a very closed person even though my personality and position may suggest otherwise. I don't like talking to others about my issues, and I quickly and easily shut down when faced with my struggles. As a pastor I have to be very careful how to share and how much I share with my sheep so that my transparency doesn't hinder the Word of God. Well, God quickly gave me the recipe. The Word of God says that God sees everything—the open and the hidden things—so I figured there are two people in this life that know everything I struggle with, and since they know I might as well be real with them. Those two people are God and me. That's right, the two people you never have to lie to and can always be real with are yourself and God.

The worst thing a person can do is lie to himself and God. To tell himself it's all right when it hasn't been. To say God understands as if that means he accepts it. To deny to yourself the issues and struggles that you know exist is death to your own victory. You have to learn how to deal with yourself and how to let God deal with you. The fact is that when you deal with yourself and admit truth, you might find some ugly things, and you may deal with some hurtful memories and rough emotions, but the only way to conquer them is to deal with them. I love the relationship between God and David because they were always honest with each other. David, in conversation with God, requested a clean heart, which means that at some point his heart got contaminated and cluttered with ugliness. The beauty is that David was not afraid to admit his dirt to God. One of the greatest accomplishments of my life is establishing a relationship with God where I can strip naked, let him view all of my issues, and know that whatever he sees he will still love me. Even if I wake up with the struggle, I walk with the freedom, because I'm not in denial about what I'm fighting.

Now it's your turn to step up to the plate and be real. What are you hiding from, and why are you in denial? If you don't open up about the changes and adjustments you need to make, then your struggle will continue to have the advantage. No one is perfect, and everyone has imperfections that must be addressed if we are to reach our full potential in life. If we stand in denial of these imperfections for whatever reason, we stand no chance in defeating the challenges blocking our growth and future. When was the last time you had a face-to-face with yourself and God? When was the last time you performed an inventory check on all things that are crooked and contaminated in your own life and mind? God is already aware of what's trapped in you that needs to come out; he's just waiting for you to give him permission to operate. You have to stop suppressing hurt, ignoring pain, and turning a blind eye to faults, because they will only make your struggle worse. I guarantee you'll have more peace, strength, clarity, and hope when you face your issues, insecurities, and hurts.

Try this. Schedule a month-to-month inventory of yourself, or maybe even a week-to-week inventory. Write down all the issues, fears, concerns, and sins that you have on the inside, then take them before the Lord and iron things out. God isn't an imaginary friend; he is as real as it gets, and he desires relationship to the point where we trust him to mold us. God says in his Word, "Cast your cares on me for I care." Let us not forsake such willingness to be comforted by the Almighty. The fact of the matter is God's correction is always better than man's because it is always done for no other reason than love. When you go to God, be totally open, giving him truth from the inward part. God will respond, and he has a million ways to show you where you need to make changes.

Outside of your relationship with God, it is also great at times to have a person you trust and with whom you can just share your struggles and ask for that person's honest opinion on where they think you need adjustments. This person can be your father, mother, pastor, best friend, or relative, and as long as they can be objective, private, and do it in love, it's worth it. You don't have to share your list of struggles and issues with everybody, but you can no longer be so closed and shut up that you totally ignore the toxins in your life that need to be dealt with.

HEALING HURTS

When we think of healing, we think of it in the most positive of terms. Healing is the desired result when we have been sick or wounded. Healing in its simplest definition is the "recovery from pain or injury," something that most would desire. After we go to the doctor for our injury, or after we've have been through surgery, we are told that it will take time to heal. Therefore, almost by default, healing hurts because it takes time to heal.

It seems that the world in general has become a "microwave" generation, in which we want everything as soon as we can get it. I too, have been found guilty of desiring quick fixes with regard to money, food, relationships, ministry, and plenty more. No, there is nothing wrong necessarily with wanting something as fast as you can get it, but it's just not a reasonable expectation. There are some things in life that take time, and when we neglect this truth we do ourselves much harm. God tells us that there is seed time and then there is harvest time. Another way to think of this is that there are times when things happen and then times when the results of what has happened spring forth. For example, there comes a time when a married couple decides to have a child, so they engage in the activities that would bring this desire to pass. As a result of this there will come another time when a child is born. One time is a result of action; the other time is a result of what that action manifests. In other words, to every time there is a season. When someone close to you did you wrong, that time was the action for which a season will cause you hurt, anger, sadness, or all of the above. I truly can understand why we would want quick fixes as it pertains to eliminating sickness, hunger, frustration, poverty, and all other things that don't feel good. At the same time we have to face the reality that generally it takes a longer time to fix something than it took to cause that something.

The unfortunate reality of healing is that an injury can take place in a matter of seconds that will take months or even years to heal from. Healing takes time, sometimes much longer than we desire. The reason it hurts while you're healing is because while you're being healed you still feel the pains of the injury until you are totally healed. We have to come to terms with the fact that true healing is total healing, and until we reach "total," we will feel pain. The reason we get hurt in one relationship and then take the issues of those injuries into another relationship is because we thought we were healed. Then a situation comes up in the other relationship, and we discover we are angry, bitter, and still hurting from the past relationship. This is why we have to stop rushing healing and allow ourselves to properly heal in time. I know it doesn't feel good, and I know we wish the pain would go away, but it just doesn't work like that. Once we accept this we can begin the process of properly healing.

As a pastor and preacher I'm constantly using and losing my voice. Coupled with the fact that I have an addiction to soda I often get sore throats. Sometimes the soreness is so bad that I have to go to the doctor, and he does the famous throat gag to see if it is strep. Then after the doctor has received the results, I hear the usual: "Nope, it's not strep. It's just going to take time for the soreness to go away." So I leave the office with no medicine—just some general instructions to rest, drink fluids, and not drink any more soda. Truthfully, I leave frustrated because I always hope the doctor will give me something that will make the pain go away quickly. The reality is I have to deal with the pain until it goes away, but with the understanding that if I do those simple things that the doctor suggests and not aggravate the situation by drinking pop and yelling, it will go away. Just because healing will take time doesn't mean it will take forever. Our pain will heal, but not if we continue to do things that interrupt the process.

Healing hurts, not only because of the amount of time it takes, but also because of the things you will have to do in order to heal. Many times injuries that are of the result of deep wounds have to be taken care of with extreme measures for them to properly heal. Sometimes these measures result in great pain, but they are necessary for the process of healing. The Word of God says, "He was wounded for our transgression, bruised for our iniquities . . . *and by his stripes we are healed*" (Isaiah 53:5). In order for us to properly heal, Jesus had to receive stripes, which suggests to me there is no true healing that won't hurt. Many of us are suffering hurt emotionally, physically, and mentally that will not heal until we are willing to accept the hurt that comes along with it. Are there people in your life who continually injure you? Until you let those people go, you can't heal properly. Very likely you don't want to let them go because it will hurt you to do so, but this really just says you don't want to be healed. Similarly, there are probably some credit cards that you know you need to totally get rid of but haven't, because it will hurt you that you won't be able to spend at moments of impulse. This says you don't really want healing from financial struggles.

There are some people you need to forgive and others that you need to confront, but fear of things becoming worse or nothing changing keeps you from acting. I'm here to tell you that you are denying yourself true healing because you won't take the extreme measures that you must take for fear that it will hurt. Well, again, healing hurts, so deal with it—that is, deal with the hurt so you can get to the healing. If you avoid the hurt you'll never obtain the healing. Yes, some things are just hard to do, but there are things that are just necessary to do. Surely it was hard for the Son of God to wrap himself up in the humanity of flesh, but it was also necessary for him to do so for the healing and salvation of man. Doing the necessary things could very well decrease the time that it takes to bring healing.

Again, it's not just healing that we want: it's *total* healing, for a halfway-healed wound is not good enough. I've discovered that a wounded person is easier to counsel and help than one whose wound has healed but not totally. Sometimes the worst thing we can do with an injury is to start feeling better, thinking that it means we are no longer injured. When we get a portion of healing we let our guard down again; we recklessly stop doing the necessary things which will keep us out of similar situations that cause injury. This is why we stay in unhealthy or dangerous relationships for years and years, because somehow a moment of make-up makes us forget years of injury and tragedy. The attitude you must take is: I'm not healed until I'm *totally* healed. I'm not delivered until I'm *totally* delivered. I'm not saying you can't celebrate progress, but I am saying you can't be satisfied until completion. Stop trying to heal overnight, and start doing everything you can and need to do in order to become totally healed.

One of the most important ingredients for becoming totally healed is first becoming totally tired with being wounded. The fact is that if you keep throwing yourself in the fire, you will continue to get burned. Every time you are reinjured it makes it harder to recover. In order for your wounds and bruises to heal, at some point you're going to have to stop reinjuring them. One of the main reasons this happens to us is because we give people the control to reinjure us, and we tend to blame a person for what they do to us and ignore that we allowed them to do it. While you can't always control what people do, you don't have to stay in a position where they can do it to you. I've often wondered as I counsel people why they stay in cycles of abuse, and I've discovered that they have a greater attachment to chains than they do to freedom. An example of this is a man who has been stuck in a dark cave for three years, only seeing darkness. When he finally escapes the cave and walks into the sun he will quickly close his eyes to hide from the brightness of the light. The reality is that when you've been in something so long, the opposite of that thing can be very uncomfortable and shocking and cause you to go back to what you're familiar with, even if it hurts you. Sometimes fear will cause us to choose what is common to us even if it is not best for us. To the addict, drugs are common and understood, and although not a healthy life choice, drugs answer the addict's need. If the addict goes into rehab and has no fixes for a few days, he may very well go into withdrawal, sweats, and pain, because while that clean state is best for him, it's not common to him.

What we have to do as it pertains to our struggle is to seek out what is best and deny what is common. If financial struggle is common to you, you might have to do some things that hurt, but you're best to let some unnecessary spending leisure and entertainment go. We have to remember that nothing becomes common until it becomes repetitive, so the things that are good for you will become common to you if you continue to do them. We have to forgo the acceptance of halfway healings. We cannot be satisfied until the struggle is over, and the wounds are totally healed.

It Happens to the Best of Us

"It happens to the best of us." You usually hear this very common phrase in regard to some negative or undesirable situation that has happened to someone as an acknowledgement that it could have or has happened to many others. When dealing with struggle it is very important that we remember this statement and apply it at least emotionally in our own dealings with struggle. A very common response to struggle is the feeling of isolation and loneliness, the perception that we are the only one going through it. This is a very dangerous way to think or even feel because it leads to an overwhelming feeling of hopelessness and abandonment. One of the greatest things that another person can do for you in your struggle is to remind you that whatever you're dealing with, somebody has been there, done that, and overcome it. On the other hand, the worst thing you can do is pity someone's situation as if what they are struggling with is uncommon to man. Agreement about the wrong things will only add fuel to an already out-of-control fire.

I'm reminded of the Scripture found in 1 Peter 4:12 which states, "Think it not strange concerning the fiery trial that is to try you, as though some strange thing happen to you." Of course someone going through a particularly hard time will probably not want to hear that Scripture, but the reality is that it would benefit more sufferers if received with the proper understanding. The Scripture itself points to the fact that things that happen to some of us happen to most of us, and our outlook on our struggle shouldn't be looked at as strange. If we look at Americans as divided into financial classes, only one percent is rich. The rest is therefore not considered rich, so for most of us, not being a millionaire is not a strange thing. In a Bible study at my church, I asked all the married couples to stand up and all the singles to stand up, and the room was pretty much split in half. I did this to point out to the single person who feels he or she is the only one who is single that perception is not always reality. The outlook on life changes dramatically when you realize that you're not the only pea in the pod. Jesus knew this when he dealt with the woman caught in the act of adultery. A group of people, including scribes and Pharisees, brought the accused adulteress to Jesus. They were all prepared to stone her, as the law dictated. As she was brought alone, the woman surely felt alone and fearful for what would happen to her, since those who had accused her also stood also awaiting her death. To test Jesus and see what he would say, they challenged him with the law of Moses, which said to stone a person caught in this act. When Jesus finally responded, he asked the group of accusers to take a different outlook on the situation and to first examine themselves. If they had no sin, then they could rightfully stone the woman for hers. At this point, every accuser was convicted by his own conscience. The crowd dropped their rocks, turned around, and dispersed. Essentially what Jesus pointed out through this story is while we may not all have done the exact same morally reprehensible things, we have all certainly done *something*. When you think you're the only one who's sinned, it's easy to feel helpless. In this story, Jesus changed the crowd's outlook and brought the realization that everyone has something they're dealing with.

Now don't get me wrong. I'm not saying that the fact that my neighbor has the same illness I do makes my illness less painful. What I am saying is the fact that my neighbor has the same illness I do lets me know I have somebody to identify with and that there is no need to feel like "it's just me." When I am aware that struggle hits everyone at some point, then I know it's not me against the world, but rather me against my struggle. I think you stand a greater chance of defeating your personal struggle than challenging the world.

The "I-mode" is what I call falling into the trap of "it's just me." This is when we preface everything we say with the word "I." *I* feel lost. *I* feel like he shouldn't have done that. *I* feel lonely. *I* feel like no one accepts me. *I* feel like an outcast. *I* feel like *I* can't make it. *I* feel like you should have been there. When we find ourselves in a state of "I," we must quickly remove ourselves from this mode. The truth is we don't have enough control of what goes on, in, and around our lives to claim such isolation and feelings of abandonment. There are so many things going on in this world, so many elements, spirits, and other forces that are out of our control that if we look at life from an "I" perspective, our vision will surely be obscured.

For example, let's say you have a picnic planned for the day, and you wake up to discover that it is raining. The "I" perspective will have you mad and frustrated and somehow feeling that the rain was sent just to mess up your day. When we begin to feel overwhelmed, unfairly attacked, frustrated, disappointed, and rejected, it is always better to look at it from a "why and what" perspective rather than "I." *Why* and *what* are much easier to evaluate and answer than "I" or "me" because the former search for the truth while the latter cater to emotions. The person who can't wait to have a picnic but discovers it's raining will look through the "I" lens to find out why it always rains on their parade. But they won't find satisfaction or an answer because what they are really saying is that they feel trapped, and the only way to cope is to feel like the rain is their personal enemy. On the other hand, the person who looks at the situation through the lens of *why* and *what* asks, "Why is it raining, and what can I do about it?" Well, the "why" it's raining is because it's part of our weather system, and whether I wanted to have a picnic or not it would have rained today. The "what" speaks to how the person should deal with the situation: "I can wait until it stops raining, or plan a picnic for another day." The why and what seek to find resolution; the "I" seeks to satisfy the individual's emotions through pity. This is why it's so hard to teach, develop, and break through to people who are stuck in I-mode: they aren't really interested in the why and what—they are looking more for your agreement. It's all about them, or else they feel you're against them. A person who says, "I'm always broke," will probably never have sufficient finances because they are so caught up in the feeling of being broke that they never address the reasons for their financial situation or search for the resolution. A person who asks, "Why am I broke and what can I do about it?" stands a greater chance of breaking out of financial struggle, because she is more interested in the solution than the emotion. I like to say struggle has no end where it has a friend—in other words, misery loves company. If you're in a struggle, don't befriend it by becoming emotionally attached to it, associating it with who you are, or allowing it to push you into I-mode. Your struggle will be over as soon as you find the solution, so before you sleep with "I," try dancing with *why* and *what*.

One very important fact that you must remember is that everyone has struggles that they deal with and have to overcome. One key element of overcoming your struggle is not connecting with those who believe they have none. I caution you to run as fast as you can from the individual or couple that tells you they never struggle in their faith, relationship, health, or career. The Word of God states that all have sin and come short of the glory of God. It also states that if God doesn't shorten the days of the Lord's return, even the very elect will be lost. Both of these statements seem to suggest we all at one time have struggled with sin, and most of us will continue to struggle as the trials and wickedness of the world grow worse. The fact is that struggle shows up at every door, sits on every couch, sleeps in every bed, and showers in every bathroom. I'm sure that there are many throughout this world who have overcome great struggles, but it is very dangerous to identify with someone who claims no struggle at all. Even the denial of struggle is a great struggle in itself.

Likewise, you don't want to connect with people who only talk about their struggle as if they are in love with it. Every time you see them they tell you about what they are going through and what just happened to them. If you allow yourself to be connected to drama then drama eventually becomes a part of your life, and surely you don't want that. So who do you need to connect with? People who are like Paul would be a good start. In Philippians 4, Paul testifies that he has learned how to be content in any situation, and that he knows how to abound and suffer. This statement by Paul shows that he is real enough to admit that he has been through many different circumstances and has suffered through struggles. The fact that he states he had to learn suggests that he was interested in the why, what, and how of overcoming a struggle rather than focusing on the emotions of what he was going through. Last but not least, Paul's ability to be content in every situation, even if not totally satisfied, points to the fact that he refused to allow the struggle to control his life. When you're going through a struggle you need real people who won't deny they have struggles, but can teach you because they've learned themselves how to cope and how to not allow the struggle to possess the control.

Always remember: it's not just you. God is aware that we all have struggles, and he will never single you out to struggle alone. We all might go through different things but we all go through something, and it's important to know that you are not alone in the struggle. Even so, we don't want people to "struggle with" but rather to "overcome with." Never join the struggle team; hook up with the overcomers' team.

Never Doubt the Opposition of Your Struggle

It depresses me that I have to tell this next story as an example of this chapter's theme. At the very least, I pretty much know that my "man card" will be revoked.

The story begins with a challenge from one of the church ministers to battle in tug-o-war at the church picnic—men versus the women. The minister who proposed the challenge was a woman and absolutely felt that the women of the church could challenge and defeat the men. I quickly suggested she back down in her challenge, stating that it wouldn't be worth the attempt because the men would win. Yep, that was me, going with the whole "men are just physically stronger than women" stereotype. However, the minister making the challenge boldly proclaimed that the women could and would win, so I happily and confidently accepted the challenge.

The day of the picnic we get to the park. I'm talking my jazz and in no way believe that the women stand a chance of beating the men. The men assembled at one end of the rope and the women at the other end. The women gathered together as if they were planning some type of strategy; we men just shrugged it off and stood there with our macho demeanor. I'm sure you've guessed by now that—and I admit this with great disgust—the women almost effortlessly pulled the men across the line. The moral of this embarrassing story is never doubt the opposition of your struggle.

The Bible declares that the Devil is not only our Enemy, but one who plans and strategizes our demise. The Bible gives us a view of the Enemy as a roaring lion stalking about and seeking whom he may devour. Just because the power of God gives us strength over the Enemy, it doesn't give us the right to be ignorant of his devices or power. Yes, the Bible declares that the weapons of the Enemy will form but not prosper, but this is not an automatic truth—rather, it is subjective. In other words, if you are not properly protected under the will of God and walking in the Spirit as opposed to the flesh, then the weapons of the Enemy can absolutely destroy you. It's like a boxer whose superiority over his opponent in ability, strength, height, and weight causes him to let his guard down thinking he can't be hurt, and then out of nowhere the opponent catches him off guard and sends him to the mat. The Enemy is no match for the believer, unless the believer's guard is down, and then the believer is no match for the Devil. Why would the Word of God encourage us to put on the whole armor so that we can defeat the Enemy, if God felt we didn't need it?

You must not underestimate the Devil and his dedication to destroying your life. As Jesus declares, the Devil's only mission is to steal, kill, and destroy. It is my belief that generally we don't take seriously enough Satan's full-throttle approach to destroying our lives, nor do we recognize that he is patient enough to see it done. The Enemy, though stupid for challenging the Almighty God, is not ignorant when it comes to his job of deception, lying, thievery, and death. In fact, the Enemy is a professional when it comes to robbing people of their callings and destinies; after all, he has been doing this for centuries and beyond. I say this to give you a clear perspective as to why you have had so many challenges in your life throughout the years: it's because you have an opposition that won't quit until you quit. The Enemy attacked Jesus at birth through the arms of King Herod, and when he didn't succeed, continued to make attempts throughout Jesus' life until he was crucified. It's no different with you. The Enemy has had a plan to destroy you by whatever means necessary, and he won't stop until his plan is fulfilled.

The Bible declares that we wrestle not against flesh and blood but against spiritual wickedness, principalities, and darkness. The great deception is that the Enemy generally hides behind the person or situation that we are faced with to defeat us. However, we can't continue to allow him to fool us and accomplish his purpose through our blindness. I'm not suggesting that every bad thing that happens to us through the arms of men or circumstance is of the Devil. Some bad things are products of life, our own actions, or even God. What I am suggesting is that we have to discern when the Enemy is using people and situations to hide behind to accomplish his true purpose. One great example of this is Samson, who was the strongest man physically in the Bible. Samson's strength lay in his obedience to God to never shave his head. The Enemy desired to find out where Samson's strength lay so he could defeat him. Thus, the Devil created a plan through the eyes and touch of a woman named Delilah. Delilah used a relationship to rob Samson of the information that if his hair was cut then he would lose his strength. Samson went to sleep with only Delilah in the room, but awoke surrounded by the Enemy, with his hair shaven and strength gone. I point this out to show that the Enemy will use people until he accomplishes his purpose, then he shows up to bind you. Not only should you not underestimate the Devil, but you cannot ignore the people and situations that make themselves available for his usage. The fact is there are some people that you just have to stop associating with because they allow the Enemy's purpose to be fulfilled through your relationship or friendship with them. There are some places that you just can't go, and even when your intentions are good and justified the environment is still an opportunity for the Enemy to distract you. The worst thing you can say is, "I'm strong enough to handle it." While that might be true, it is better to be wise enough to avoid it. Wisdom is greater than strength because strength can become prideful trying to lift and push everything while wisdom won't allow strength to be tested unnecessarily. In other words, don't try to prove you can defeat temptation; rather, try to be wise enough not to put yourself in the way of temptation. And if temptation does find you, believe that you are strong enough to defeat it on your own turf.

Now I wish I could say that the Devil is the only opposition that we have to worry about. Sadly, that is simply not the case. There are many challenges in life that we have to be aware of and not take lightly or we will find it harder to be successful. Daily we face things such as fear, insecurities, doubt, lack of a parent, past failures, mistakes, bad decisions, broken relationships, sickness, disabilities, wayward children, and so many other oppositions. It becomes very easy to begin to see these things as just a part of life as opposed to the oppositions in your life that are keeping you from reaching your full potential. I believe that it is essential for you to keep this mindset: anything that prohibits me from reaching my all is my opposition, and I have to defeat it. Something as simple as a poor attitude can keep you from reaching higher levels in life. You have to be willing to defeat the opposition at all costs—even if the opposition is you. Never become comfortable with things that are against you; instead, turn them into your victories by overcoming them and using them to your advantage. After suffering defeat at the church picnic—even though it was a friendly competition—I decided never again to doubt the opposition in front of me. We must always give greater intensity to overcoming our struggle than our struggle gives to defeating us. The moment we doubt the opposition in our lives is the moment we lose the advantage.

WHEN IT WON'T LET YOU GO, LET IT GO

Let's get right to it: there are some things holding on to you because you are holding on to them. You're dreaming about something because you're thinking about it; you're crying over it because you're still connected to it; you keep falling for it because you're still open to it. At some point other people and the issue itself have to stop being the excuses for why, year after year, you never get over your struggle.

Two of the greatest pains in life are guilt and shame, but greater than these is self-guilt. The condemnation of oneself is worse than the condemnation of others. It is very painful as a pastor to watch people struggle with guilt and self-condemnation. God has delivered them from the bondage of their past sins and failures, yet they are trapped in the memory of what they used to do and who they used to be. Equally painful is watching people who are trapped in situations that they inwardly hate but outwardly find hard to escape. There are plenty of women in physically, mentally, and emotionally abusive relationships, and even though they hate the abuse, they find it easier to stay than to leave. The man who grew up without a father hates that he didn't have a male figure in his life and struggles to not repeat the same behavior of having children he can't parent. How many times have you heard a child say, "When I grow up I'm going to be nothing like my mother or father," and then somehow the child ends up turning out exactly like his or her parents. I believe much of this seemingly backward struggle is due to the fact that we hold on to so much negativity—evils, hurts, failures, regrets, behaviors—that we end up embracing the things we dislike the most. Have you ever met a person who says they hate drama and can't stand when people get in their business, yet they tell everyone about all of their business and thus create drama? Or even better, the person who says their life is a mess, yet fails to realize that the majority of the mess was caused by their own doings and decisions. One great way to defeat cycles in your life such as these is to let go, stop battling, and start fresh.

Some people are truly afraid to let go, fearful of forgiving others or even themselves. Sometimes the unknown seems too risky a move to step into. I am of the belief that the unknown can't be worse than the pain and suffering that most of us endure by hanging on to what has already been. Life is about moving forward; those who stay tied to the past or stuck in the now miss out on the greatness of their future. Is the "ex" who hurt you really worth the constant talking and thinking about what they did to hurt you and ruin your life? Nine times out of ten the ex has already moved on with their life; it's time that you moved on with yours. God is a forgiving God who moves to the next step and doesn't allow his dislike of our sin to cause us to miss out on future blessings. We should take note from him! If people hold you accountable to a past that you have already turned from, then shame on them, but if you allow it to make you think twice about the changes you've made and the new person you have become, shame on you. We have to stop allowing disgruntled and bitter people to bind us to their issues; if you've moved on, then don't look back. Don't allow the hurts and pains that others caused to have the victory over you by wanting revenge. The greatest payback you can have is rising above the dirt others have thrown on you.

Most of us know that even though we won't admit it, when it's time to let go of something, the difficulty is in the actual letting go. Many times in the midst of wanting to let go it may seem so hard to do that we kind of freak ourselves out and just allow the struggle to continue. The first step to letting something go is moving past the fear to walk away; once the fear has been quenched the walk will be easy. I often use the example of the dog that comes running around the corner at you full speed, barking furiously, teeth bared. Your mind and heart may say *Run!* but fear many times will place you in shock and cause you to stand still. Fear freezes you, and in order to move on you have to break out of the ice of fear and step into the fire of freedom. Don't allow the fear to freeze you; instead, allow the prospect of being free from struggle to set you a burning flame, and just walk away.

What exactly am I telling you to walk away from? Most people hear "you need to walk away" and generally associate that with a relationship. The statement could apply if the relationship is causing a cycle of struggle and preventing you from your greatness, but relationships are not the only things we need to walk away from. Many of us need to walk away from sin, addiction, people, attitudes, bad habits, doubt, the past, and so much more. The thing to do is sit down and determine exactly what you need to walk away from, and then make the choice to do so. The next step is making sure that when you walk away from something that you are really ready to let go, because if you're still holding on to it while you're walking away, it's just going with you. Letting go means totally ridding yourself of what you've been holding on to. Easier said than done? Of course—most things are. But again, just because something may be hard doesn't mean it is not necessary. Time moves too fast for us to be moving so slowly to let go and walk away. In other words, while you're patiently taking your time to make the right decision, you're only allowing for more struggle to pile up and weigh you down. We must remember that struggle is not patient; it is constant. Therefore, you must make haste to rid yourself of at least of the parts that you control.

I don't profess to be a psychic so I can't tell you that the grass will be greener on the other side when you walk away. I can't tell you that you won't run into any more struggles after you let this one go, because more than likely that won't be the case. What I can say with surety is that those who refuse to get comfortable in struggle develop a clear mindset and work ethic: no matter what the struggle is, they will overcome it. So, if you walk away and later find yourself in another struggle, you won't stay there because you never want to be bound again. If there is any benefit of going through negative situations, it's the experience that allows you to know how it feels and gives you the power to deny it the next time it confronts you. If I allow someone to borrow money from me with the promise that they will give it back, and they do not, I might feel taken advantage of, upset, confused, and maybe a little angry. The good thing is now I have the power the next time that person asks me for money to tap into my experience of what happened, and how I felt the last time they asked, and I said yes. My response would be an overwhelming "no" because I never want to put myself in the same position where I would feel badly like the first time.

You may be asking yourself, "So the fact that good or bad can happen to me in the future doesn't exempt me from the reality that I'll never know what's up the road if I stay stuck on the side?" The power of motion works against the power of struggle, in that struggle seeks to stop me. So if I can walk away from the struggle, I defeat its purpose. In more simplistic terms I'm saying that letting go and walking away will work in your favor. Letting go and walking away from the struggles that you've been holding on to for years will give a sense of peace and change that will now allow you to be optimistic about your future, as opposed to staying bound to a struggle that has up until this point only held you back and hurt you.

Paul showed that he understood the power of forward motion in Philippians 3:13 where he states, he forgets that which is behind him and reaches for what's in front of him. The further you get away from your struggle, the less control it has over your life. Consider the story of Lot and his family who were in the wrong place at the wrong time. God was getting ready to destroy Sodom and Gomorrah but allowed space for Lot and his family to leave before the destruction. The angel told Lot and his family to make haste and to not look back. As they began to leave, Lot's wife made the mistake of looking back and was turned into a pillar of salt. Lot and his children escaped because they kept moving forward; his wife got stuck because she looked back.

Instead of continually holding on to things that keep you stuck, how about trying to let them go by moving forward? Forward motion puts greater distance between you and what's in the rearview.

RISE ABOVE THE STRUGGLE: BEAST MODE

The mark of greatness is determined by the depth of the struggle. I would even go so far as to suggest that one can't be great without struggle. Jesus is great above all: he faced the greatest struggle but rose above it. Other great leaders such as Martin Luther King Jr., Rosa Parks, the apostle Paul, Job, Nelson Mandela, and a host of others were great—not simply because of what they accomplished, but rather what they accomplished through struggle. Sadly, not everyone has the persuasive fortitude to say to their struggle: "You are just the ladder that God has placed in my life for me to climb and reach my destiny."

You want greatness? Well, it comes with a price. Can you pay the cost? I believe that you can, and I believe that if *you* believe, then you will. It's not good enough just to survive; you've been surviving for a long time. Now you have to shift into "beast mode." What is beast mode? It is like being Popeye or the Incredible Hulk: in their natural forms they can do a little, but when struggle comes, they take on another form that allows them to conquer. It's time for you to shift forms! Don't just let your struggle challenge you—challenge your struggle. If your struggles have been defeating you for years then challenge yourself that this will be the last year. Instead of "settling" and accepting that your life is never going to really get better, let the beast come out and allow you to rise above the struggle. Everyone has that beast in them, but sometimes he has to be pushed out.

Remember the woman in the Bible with the issue of blood? She had been suffering for twelve years. She had lost all her money, the doctors misused her, and even with all of their medicine the sickness just grew worse. It got to the point where nothing else could be done for the woman, and it seemed that all hope was lost. But the woman refused to give up so easily. She heard that Jesus was passing through and believed that if she got to him she could be healed. However, there were a few issues. For one thing, she was a sick lady, and Jesus was surrounded by a great throng. How was she going to get to him? In addition, Jesus was actually at the time on his way to heal a ruler's daughter, so it seemed he was already occupied. Would the woman risk interrupting his mission? She weighed her options and saw that the odds were not in her favor; therefore, she decided that to get things done she would have to go into beast mode. With no other choice the woman gave her all and set out to get what she was looking for, regardless of how hard it would be. She pressed through the crowd that was thronging against Jesus, no doubt being bumped and banged around, and kept pushing until eventually she made it. She stretched out and reached her target, Jesus, and was rewarded for her faithfulness by being healed. Why should it be any different for you? Things are already difficult, so what are you afraid of? When you refuse to stand still and do nothing you stand a greater chance of things getting better. The time is now! There is no more time to waste, for wasted time is death inching closer. You must move with haste and tap into the greatness inside you. Tap into the willpower that was given to you from creation to push beyond your human limits and go into the supernatural. The struggle is only as strong as you allow it to be. It doesn't easily go away but it will bow out if you rise up.

Again I ask: Who do you know who has achieved greatness without struggle? Barack Obama, the first African-American president of the United States, achieved one of the greatest accomplishments in the history of America and did so in the face of struggle, challenged daily about his faith, birthplace, ideas, race, and love for the country he serves. He stood in adversity and rose to victory. It wasn't easy but it was necessary if he wanted to accomplish something that had never been done in presidential history. Obama's act of bravery and willingness to challenge the struggles he faced changed the scope in which we view all men as having equal opportunity to excel on every level of this society. I hope that you realize that your own act of bravery and willingness to do the same will change the outlook on your life, too. Those connected to you will also see the change. The stance you take now will set the path for generations upon generations of your bloodline to see success without going through the struggles you had to overcome.

Many of us believe that we are doing what we need to do simply because we haven't given up, and while that is good it is only half of the battle. The struggle of our lives won't end because we keep getting up when they knock us down; a bully will only quit when you strip him of his control over you. You have to strip your struggle of its control, and you do this by giving it no ammunition to shoot at you. Rising above your struggle can simply mean going back to school, applying for that higher position, forgiving someone, starting a business, changing your attitude, refusing to quit, taking a stand, taking control—whatever it is, just do it. Struggles exist at every level, but the victory is in overcoming them, and I am here to tell you that it is possible with a determined mind. Your life will no longer be dictated by your struggle; instead, your struggle will be dictated by your desire to overcome it. Success is not in your struggle, but it's in front of it. Press on and move forward.

OVERCOMING STRUGGLE

Struggle doesn't end when you get up, but rather when you knock it down. I want you to take the next few seconds to imagine a life without any struggle. Take a couple more seconds to view that life without anything trying to stop you. Now, doesn't that feel good? Okay, now I want you to snap out of it and wake up, because that is the only time you won't have struggle. The fact is that struggle is always present, even when it's hidden. Even when it has yet to poke its head out and grab you, it's present. We have to stop imagining a life without struggle, start standing up to all struggles that challenge us, and overcome them. Jesus, in Revelation, makes a list of statements that he will give to his people if they overcome. These "overcoming" statements by Jesus are so important because they stress the fact that when you overcome, great things happen to you. I don't need you to imagine a life without struggle, I need you to overcome struggle so you can receive all the things that your struggles are hindering. Yes, I know it's easier said than done (most things are), but again: it may not be easy but it is necessary. The greatness in you is dependent on the willingness to overcome your struggle. How many times do we quote the Scripture "I am more than a conqueror," but miss the point? The only way you can be a conqueror is if you overcome something or someone, and the only way to be more than that is to overcome consistently.

FOREWORD

In 2010, Pastor William Bennett completed his first book, *Winners Play With Pain*. He is back with an inspiring revelation on how to overcome struggle in *The Struggle With Struggle*. Some struggle is obvious; other struggle is so deep-rooted that sometimes we just can't see it for what it is. Bennett's new book is filled with instructions on how to overcome real life struggles and how to identify and defeat the things that are trying to defeat you. *The Struggle With Struggle* is a book for everyone. If you have some form of struggle in your life, it's time to overcome.

ABOUT THE AUTHOR

Pastor William has a gift from God to write material that will speak to the many life challenges people face everyday as was seen in his first book "Winners Play with Pain". Now authoring his second book "The Struggle with Struggle" Pastor Bennett shows that he is young enough but wise enough to present a message that feeds all ages, genders, races, and prompts the reader to make successful changes. Pastor William has been in the church all of his life born to Pastor Andrew and Colleen Bennett; he is anointed and appointed to lead and speak to a generation such as this. Pastor Bennett thrives off of his desire to help people become the person God created them to be, he believes that circumstances are not an excuse to live beneath ones ability. He has a passion and drive to minister the Word of God and deliver encouragement that will bring healing and faith to all. Pastor Bennett is the Senior Leader of the City of Refuge church located in Bloomington, IL and has seen first hand the power of God who miraculously led the church from a 4800sft building into its current place of worship over 27,000sft. All who come in contact with this great man of God are instantly affected and moved in themselves to achieve better.

Printed in the United States
By Bookmasters